Mike's

HOW TO START
AN ONLINE BUSINESS
(FOR UNDER $10)

*"How I make a full-time living working
just a few hours per week
...and you can too!"*

$10,000

MIKE STAPLETON

MIKE'S MONEY METHOD

HOW TO START AN ONLINE BUSINESS
(FOR UNDER $10)

MIKE STAPLETON

Mike's Disclaimer

Income Disclaimer: This book contains business strategies, marketing methods and other business advice that has worked for me, but depending on your own effort and life experience, may not produce the same results for you. I make absolutely no guarantee, expressed or implied, that you will make any money by following this advice. I don't know you and there are simply too many factors and variables regarding your situation that I'm not aware of.

Liability Disclaimer: By taking my advice, you assume all risks involved with the full understanding that you are solely responsible for anything that may occur as a result of putting this information into action in any way, and regardless of your interpretation of the advice.

You further agree that I cannot be held responsible in any way for the failure of your business as a result of the information presented. There are too many variables for me to get involved like that. Because of this, I'm leaving it up to you to conduct your own due diligence regarding the safe and successful operation of your business if you intend to apply any of my information in any way to your business operations.

In summary, you understand that I make absolutely no guarantees regarding income as a result of applying this information, as well as the fact that you are solely responsible for the results of any action taken on your part as a result of this information.

ISBN: 978-0-9811437-7-4

Mike Stapleton
Suite 264
2 Toronto St.
Toronto, ON Canada
M5C 2B5

INTRODUCTION

If someone were to ask me, "Out of all the online money-making strategies you've learned and used over the years, if you were only allowed to use **one** strategy from this day forth, which strategy would you choose – and why?"

Without even blinking, I would have to say article marketing. If I had to pick only one strategy to use, and nothing else for the rest of my life, I would choose article marketing.

If you could have one of your articles published on more than 400 different Web sites, in a matter of weeks, so that they all continued to bring in more traffic, subscribers, and sales for you, on complete autopilot, how many more articles would you attempt to do that with?

This is my favorite traffic strategy because it is quick, easy, free, and it can continue to work for you *indefinitely*, without you having to do any additional work.

If you are anything like I was when I first started attempting to make money online, you're probably ready to pull your hair out. Although there is a ton of information available that can tell you what you need to do, attempting to sort through it all without experiencing information overload is next to impossible.

What you are about to read is a step-by-step process that will allow you to take the guesswork out of the equation.

I am going to show you how to use article marketing as a quick and easy way to begin making money online. It doesn't matter if you are a good writer because you can find people to write articles for you or find articles that have already been written. You don't even have to know how to set up a Web site because you can post your articles on other sites and leverage the high traffic those sites receive.

By no means is this the *only* way to make money on the Internet. There are thousands of different paths you can choose. Some require more work than others and some cost more money than others. The way I am about to show you is one that will not cost you a dime of your own money if you do not want it to. These methods can be followed by using strictly free resources. You, of course, can speed up the process by spending a little bit of your own money, but it is by no means necessary.

Of all the ways to make money online, in my opinion, article marketing is the easiest and best way for anybody to make their first dollar.

The best part is, that without spending anymore than the cost of a domain name and Web hosting (which would be $9 for the domain and $5/month for hosting), you can create a passive income that can bring you money from an article you wrote and will bring you income for years to come.

So ask yourself, is spending a few minutes writing a 250-word article worth the time if it continues to bring you money years later?

Yeah, I thought "yes" would be the answer.

There are many different opinions on how you should approach article marketing. No matter what anyone tells you when it comes down to it, you should always be thinking about how to best give your reader value by offering them informative articles. If you give your reader information they can use, the chances of them buying the product you're attempting to sell increases dramatically.

Benefits of Article Marketing

One strategically designed and positioned article can continue to bring in more and more highly targeted traffic (and profits) over time, without any extra work.

Unlike most traffic strategies, your traffic flow from articles can continue to increase on its own.

You can immediately get listed on high-traffic, highly ranked and respected sites, and benefit from *their* popularity and traffic. (They *want* you to list your articles on their site.)

Any one of your articles can be picked up by another source/publisher and increase your exposure/traffic even more. (You get exposed to all of *their* readers and customers immediately, and you get to borrow their credibility and status.)

And, of course, by posting an article on an authority site, you can be seen as an expert in your field. (That is a great position to be in.)

Article marketing is a popular way to make money online.

Unfortunately, as popular as this strategy is, it is also one of the most misunderstood and misused strategies out there. Most people who use this strategy see mediocre to poor results.

Contrary to what many people think, article marketing is not about bombarding the Internet with as many articles as you can possibly churn (or spin) out. There's a little more to it than that.

When used correctly, each article that you publish can become an ongoing traffic – and profit – source, earning you anywhere from $50 – to $500 (or more) per month. That's *per article.*

If you are willing to put in the time to follow this method, you will likely make money and, hopefully, make a good amount of it

What you need to remember is that there is no superhighway to making money on the Internet. You **must** stay consistent and motivated even when you get frustrated and feel like things are not going your way. It is those who continue to work and promote their business that will in the end be successful.

I wish you the greatest of success! Work hard and follow this workbook and you'll be on your way faster than you would have ever thought possible.

PART ONE: Getting Started

CHAPTER ONE: Where's the Money? Picking a Niche Made Easy

When it comes to article marketing, most people start out by not knowing what to write about. You want to write about something that interests you and that you can write about with confidence, but you also want to pick a popular niche that will increase your chances of making money.

Here's an easy method I have used to find many great niches.

First and most importantly, ask yourself:

Is there a problem that someone really needs a solution to?

Think about that for a minute. If a person has a problem and they are looking for a solution, they will almost definitely buy something that will give them a solution. Your job is to use articles to convince them you can provide that solution.

In my opinion, offering a solution to a problem is much more profitable than providing information about a hobby or a curiosity. When people have problems or issues, they want answers and a solution and they want it now!

So, when picking a niche, put yourself in the position of the buyer. If you had a certain problem such as a "yeast infection" and you have been struggling with curing it for a while, would you pay for a solution? Damn right you would!

(As a side note, I chose to use curing yeast infection as an example because, as you will see when you begin to research profitable niches, it is a very popular and lucrative one for article marketers.)

Now don't confuse "wants" with "problems." Weight loss, for instance, is not necessarily a "problem." It can be a problem, but wanting to lose weight is just that; "wanting to." On the other hand, if a person has high blood pressure, that is a serious problem a person would want to fix as soon as possible.

Don't get me wrong, there is a lot of money in the "weight loss" niche, just as there is a lot of money in the "make money online" niche, but it's tough to get a consistent piece of those pies. You will do much better, and see results much faster, if you get into niches that will give people quick solutions to immediate problems.

Problems (and their solutions) can be found in many niches beyond health and wellness. If a person is really into video games but can't seem to get past a certain level, they have a problem. They will be willing to pay if you can provide them a way to get past that level. Here are other examples of problems for which people are looking for solutions:

- panic attacks
- skin tabs
- heartburn

- suspecting your spouse is cheating
- playing basketball and not being able to jump very high
- having a virus on your computer
- tinnitus (constant ringing in the ear)

Find the niches in which people are desperate for a solution to a problem and you'll find the money you are looking for!

One great Web site to find problems people are being burdened with is Yahoo Answers (answers.yahoo.com). I highly suggest you start your research there.

Clickbank

Once you've thought of a problem, it's time to visit Clickbank (clickbank.com). Clickbank is Web site that lists "infoproducts" within their marketplace. For the buyer, it is a site to visit to find ebooks and other digital products relating to their topic of interest. For an article marketer such as yourself, it is the Web site you must visit to find out what products are already out there and what products you would like to promote.

For someone new to making money online, Clickbank is a dream come true. People have done all the hard work for you by creating a product and the sales copy to sell the product. They need people like you to get the word out about their product. For every sale you make of their product, you get a percentage of what the buyer paid. This is called "affiliate sales."

It's easy and a win-win solution for everyone.

Look within the Clickbank marketplace for a product that will solve this problem. Chances are you will find more than one. Take a look at the products offered and see which one is selling the best. You can tell which product is doing well by looking at what Clickbank calls "gravity." The higher the gravity number, the better the sales are.

Once you choose to be an affiliate of a product, you can retrieve your affiliate link for the product via Clickbank. This is the link you will use to send readers to the product page. Remember, this is called an **affiliate link** and is the most important tool you will use to connect the buyer with the product and ensure you get paid for the sale.

A Clickbank affiliate link looks something like this:

http://2br4kfjg6eydq8bff4mwckeak10.hop.clickbank.net/

Clickbank uses this link to track your sales and then sends you your earnings twice a month.

Back in the day, you could take the affiliate link Clickbank generates and include it in your articles as is. Not anymore. These days, you must buy a domain and forward your domain to your affiliate link.

You can purchase a domain for less than $10 at sites such as KRDomains.com.

Choose a domain that includes keywords associated with the niche you have chosen. (More about keyword research in the next section.)

Domain forwarding simply means that you will forward the domain you purchased to your affiliate link. This way, rather than people seeing your long, character-laden Clickbank affiliate link, they will just see your domain instead.

Not only is mandatory to have a domain appear instead of your affiliate link, more readers will click on a domain. People have more trust in a simple domain such as "teachingyoudogtraining.com" than an affiliate link. Affiliate links indicate that you want to sell something. Sometimes, when people see your motivation is for them to buy a product so you can make money, they will not click on the link.

Once you have purchased your domain, set it up so that when someone goes to that domain they will be direct to the product page you are promoting.

Getting Set Up

The next thing you are going to do is called *keyword research*. Don't worry, it's not as difficult or daunting as it may first appear.

There are many different ways to do keyword research. There are Web sites you can use and software that makes keyword research easy. Because you are keeping your expenses at a minimum, I am going to suggest two free sites: Google Adwords Tool (adwords.google.com) and the free version of WordTracker (freekeywords.wordtracker.com).

As you begin to make money with your article marketing

endeavors, you may want to invest in paying for keyword research software, but in the meantime, take comfort in knowing the Google and WordTracker resources are used widely and are excellent.

You are going to be looking for keywords people will be typing into Google to find solutions to their problems. Use your imagination, common sense and knowledge to try different words or phrases you think people would use. Once you type in your word or phrase, the results you receive will be words and phrases that go along with the one you typed in.

Make sure you put quotation marks around the phrases you are researching to ensure your search is for the exact phrase. If you don't, you will get keywords that will claim to get thousands of searches a month when in reality they don't get any.

Here is a quick way to find even more keyword ideas to use in order to find out what people with your chosen problem are searching for.

Go to the most popular article directory on the Internet: Ezine Articles (ezinearticles.com).

Look up other articles that are written about the same subject you are targeting. Once you have found an article, click on the "View" menu on the top of your browser.

The drop down box will open and you will click on the "Source" or "Page Source" option.

A new window will open that contains the HTML code for the article you were viewing. Here is an example of what you need to look for:

<meta name="keywords" content="catch a cheater">

I found this from an article about catching a cheating spouse. This particular article was targeted around the keyword "catch a cheater." You can find some great keywords or phrases this way. The grunt work has already been done for you when you use this method.

Now do another search using Ezine Articles, just as did to find other articles and the keywords they have used. Once you have a list of five or so, go back to whichever keyword research tool you were using (Google Adwords or WordTracker) and do searches using what you have found.

Once you do a search, look at the results you have gotten back. Choose the keywords that have been used the most by people doing searches.

Make a list of 10 keywords you will use. If you can find a keyword that has 60 or more searches a day and appears on less than 10,000 Web pages, you have found yourself a gold mine.

With article marketing, do not to go after a keyword or phrase that has less than 30 searches a day or appears on 900 Web pages a month. You want to invest your time in words people are searching for and ones that have some competition. On the other hand, words that appear on 35,000+ Web pages offer too much competition.

That's not saying that you can't go after a keyword phrase with such high completion. You can. But for the fastest success, keep it under 20,000. Obviously, the lower the competition the better chance you have of getting your article ranking on the front page of Google, which is how you will get the most traffic to your article.

Try and find "buying"-related keyword phrases such as "where to buy" or "get something." The more targeted you are with keywords that are "buying" keywords, the better your results.

Finally, once you have done keyword research for your product, go to Ezine Articles to create your own account so you can begin submitting your articles very soon.

20 POPULAR NICHES

Here are a list of timeless popular niches. With these topics, there will always be a demand for solutions to the problem. As an article marketer, keep in mind, you will be coming up against a great deal of competition within these niches. The best thing to do is find a niche within a niche. An example of a "niche within a niche" would be taking the "losing weight after pregnancy" niche and getting more specific to appeal to, not all women, but instead only women in their 30's who want to lose weight after pregnancy.

Check out this list to see if there are any niches you want to research further:

1. Acid Reflux
2. Get My Ex Back
3. Adult Dating
4. Yeast Infection
5. Losing Weight After Pregnancy
6. Erectile Dysfunction
7. Graves Disease
8. Bad Breath
9. Excessive Sweating
10. Penis Enlargement
11. Diabetes
12. Paid Online Work
13. High Blood Pressure
14. Male Hair Loss
15. Women's Hair Loss
16. ADHD
17. Bodybuilding
18. Acne & Blackheads
19. Forex
20. Stop Foreclosure

CHAPTER TWO: Writing Your Articles: An Easy Step-By-Step Guide

There's no hard and fast rule that says what kind of content you need to put in your article to make it most effective in getting the reader to click on the affiliate link you include. Many experienced article marketers say you must have great information in your article. Good quality information would consist of things like ideas on how to help the reader solve their problem (such as 10 ways to remove an ink stain) or an in-depth explanation of one particular solution (how baking soda can be used to remove a stain). Some article marketers believe you shouldn't give the reader *any* real information if you want to be successful –believing the less information you give them the better off you are. It may sound crazy, but it does work for some marketers.

Try to experiment with both types of articles and see which ones you get the best results from. This is the only way to tell what will work best for you.

Keep your articles short. Three hundred words per article is enough.

There are three reasons for this. The first is that you want the person reading the article to be able to see your affiliate link in the resource box no matter where they are in the article. (More on what a resource box is and placing your link in it to come.)

If your article is long, the reader will then have to scroll down to get to your affiliate link. Often times, a reader won't even finish reading before they leave the Web page.

You want the article to be short so that it is always visible while they are reading without them having to scroll down. Even if they don't finish reading the article, knowing the link is there heightens the chance they will click on it.

Second, anything more than 300 words is just too long to keep a reader's attention long enough to actually finish the article without getting bored and leaving before clicking your affiliate link. One could argue that if the article was written well and contained quality information the reader would read to the end. That's not necessarily true. The reality is, the shorter articles are more apt to lead the reader to click on your link for more information.

Third, the last thing you want to do is give out too much information. You want them to click on the affiliate link in your resource box to find out more. Within a lengthy article, there's a good bet you've given them to much information, or at least enough to make them think they can try to fix their problem on their own.

Even though they probably won't be able to solve their problem, it won't stop them from trying. Once they figure out they can't fix it themselves, the chances of them getting back to your article and clicking on your affiliate link are slim to none.

Now you can get into the actual writing of the article.

There are three parts to the article. They are:

1. The title
2. The body
3. The resource box

We'll tackle them in order and I'll show you how to get the most out of each one.

Writing The Title

The title is the most important part of the article. That might sound crazy, but the truth is, if you have a boring title, nobody is going to open your article.

When writing a title, you have to get creative. There is nothing worse than a boring title.

For this example, we're going to use "dog training" as the topic of the article. Remember, you've done your keyword research and have a list of 10 "dog training" words or phrases to choose from.

Go to your list and pick a keyword/phrase. The one you decide to use **must** go at the beginning of the title.

Having your keyword at the beginning of your title is crucial because Google seems to give you better rankings if it's at the beginning of a title rather than the end.

Next, make your title long. A long title will stand out more than a short one. If you've got a list of 15 articles, the ones with the longer titles will stand out more and not just blend in like the short ones will. Don't overlook this tip! Long titles will always get more attention than short ones. Plus you can get more creative with longer titles than short titles.

Let's use "potty training my dog" as the keyword phrase

for this example.

There are two titles below. Read them, and then ask yourself which one you would read if you were someone searching for a solution to your dog pooping where he shouldn't.

Potty Training My Dog – Nobody Likes an Untrained Dog

or

Potty Training My Dog – Steps That Will Help Keep You from Murdering Your Pet and Ensure Your Dog Never Pees On Your Couch Again

When you are creating your title, don't be scared to get a little creative with them. Here's an example of a creative title:

Get Your Ex Back With These Steps – Is Tying Them Up Included?

The more creative, and even shocking, your titles are, the more they will get read. The more normal your title, the more they look like everybody else's title and the less views you'll get.

Writing The Article Body

As mentioned before, just how informative your article content is will be up to you to test and track the results. However, for this section, I want to explain how giving little useful information within an article can work to your advantage.

If you're going to try this technique of article marketing, the rule is to hone in on the reader's deepest emotions and do not give them any information they could use, or think they could use, to solve their problem.

The product you are promoting with the affiliate link in the resource box of your article is meant to do that.

The less information you give them, the more likely they will click on the link to the product you would like them to buy. Your article must do two things:

- Speak to the emotion they are feeling by not having a solution to their problem (i.e. frustration over a misbehaving dog, embarrassment over having acne, fear over a possible cheating spouse).

- Give them a place where they can find information (your affiliate link in the resource box).

From there, you let the product's sales page do its job because that's what it's supposed to do!

Now you may think that's a little harsh, but you won't when you see money coming in! What do you think commercials on television do? If you really analyze them, they are playing on people's emotions.

You've seen commercials on TV that are selling a cure for acne. The person with the acne problem has a depressed look on their face which is meant to symbolize the feelings almost anyone suffering from acne would have.

What happens next in the commercial? You guessed it. The next frame shows this same person with a big smile on their face and exuding confidence. Why? Their acne is gone, thanks to the product being sold.

Then, of course, you are shown the product and you think, "Hey, if it worked for them, maybe it will work for me!" Now you don't know for sure if it will work, but if having acne is a big problem for you, you're going to be willing to take a chance that it will work and your feelings of dis-comfort will be relieved as well.

Notice that they don't give you any "real" information as to how it's going to work or suggestions for acne-removing methods you can try on your own. If you want to get results, your going to have to take your chances that the product is going to work. That's called good marketing and it's no different than what you're going to do with your ar-ticles.

And that's why we pick niches that have to do with solving people's problems.

Let's take the "yeast infection" niche. We know there is not a woman in the world who really wants anyone to know they are dealing with one. So, we're going to play on these facts about such a problem:

1. It is embarrassing.
2. Over the counter medications treat only the infection.

3. It can cause vaginal odor.

4. It can come back if not treated properly.

Notice how, within that list, you won't find anything that gives you any advice on how to cure it. Your article is meant to push the emotional hot buttons of the reader to evoke their need to solve this problem as soon as possible.

Below is an example of an article about yeast infections.

Example: keyword: Dealing With Vaginal Odor

Title: Dealing With Vaginal Odor - Not Only is it Embarrassing But it is Also Upsetting For a

Article body: *Dealing with vaginal odor is a very embarrassing thing for a woman to deal with. Not only is it upsetting because you have an odor coming from the most private part of your body, but it is all so embarrassing that your spouse may notice it. Just think how it can ruin a person's sexual confidence! It can also be very embarrassing having to go to the doctor to get some type of remedy. Studies show that 99% of the time, the reason a woman has vaginal odor is due to an infection. Keep reading to find out what you can do to get rid of vaginal odor.*

Most people will be run to the store and purchase an over-the-counter medication when dealing with vaginal odor. The unfortunate thing is most people do not know that these medications do nothing but treat the symptoms of an infection. Even doctor prescribed medications do nothing more than take care of the symptoms of a yeast infection.

Some of the symptoms you may have are natural odor, itching, burning, vaginal discharge and swelling. In order to get rid of vaginal odor you must treat the actual infection and not just the symptoms. Many times the actual infection is inside the intestines.

Because doctor-prescribed medications and over-the-counter remedies treat only the symptoms, the infection eventually comes back and just makes a person more upset. Because of this, thousands of women are switching to certain home remedies when dealing with vaginal odor and yeast infections.

These remedies treat the actual infection itself not only the symptoms. The results that have been reported have been extremely positive. Not only have people been getting great results, they are also able to do it from the comfort of their home saving them the embarrassment of letting someone else know they have a foul vaginal odor.

Within this example article, the reader has been reminded of their embarrassment, and told that buying over-the-counter medications and doctor prescriptions isn't going to help long term and that a lot of people are using other remedies for solutions.

We gave them no information about any method they can try to cure the yeast infection on their own. We did tell them there are "certain remedies" that have had extremely positive results and can be done at home. We've just planted the seed in their mind that all the "normal" treatments are not going to give them a permanent cure. The hope is even if the reader hasn't tried those yet, chances are they are not going to now.

Put yourself in the shoes of the person who just read this example article. If you had this problem, would you click the link in the resource box to, at least, look at the "certain remedies" that are being talked about?

I think there's a good chance you would.

Now it's time for your resource box to finish the selling job. So here's an example of the resource box that could be used to end the article and let them know there is a solution to their problem just one mouse click away.

Resource box: *If you are suffering from a yeast infection, here is my #1 recommended remedy on <u>dealing with vaginal odor.</u> This remedy gives you proven advice and guarantees that it will give you the best vaginal-odor solution possible by <u>clicking here.</u>*

Since the article keyword is "dealing with vaginal odor," you would place your affiliate link within the words "dealing with vaginal odor" as well as "clicking here," which would take the reader to the product sales page.

In summary, the article is a good template for your future articles. It's short so they can see always see the resource box, and it doesn't give them any information on how to solve their problem. It reminds them of the problems their condition is causing. We give them a place where they can find a solution to the problem: your affiliate link!

Now that we know how to write an article, let's get to the creating the perfect resource box.

Creating the Resource Box

Creating a resource box that will help not only entice your reader to click on your affiliate link, but also help your article rank higher on Google, is very important.

Once the reader has finished reading your article, their desire to find a solution to their problem will be piqued. Now your resource box must convince them to take the next step – to check out the product you are recommending.

In your resource box, take the opportunity to remind them of the problem they have and then give them a recommended solution for it.

Here's another example of a good resource box. This time we'll use the heartburn niche:

If you've had enough of dealing with constant pain of heartburn no matter how you have tried to cure it, here is my #1 recommended solution to getting rid of heartburn. Stop the constant pain caused by this condition and find a solution by clicking here.

Remember, always have your have your keyword hyperlinked in your resource box. In this case, "getting rid of heartburn" and "clicking here" both hold your affiliate link.

This is what the HTML code would look like within your resource box that would ensure your keywords are hyperlinked:

<a href="http://www.yourwebsite.com">getting rid of heartburn</a>

This is how the entire text in the resource box would look like:

If you've had enough of dealing with constant pain of heartburn no matter how you have tried to cure it, here is my #1 recommended solution to <a href="http://www.yourwebsite.com">getting rid of heatburn</a>. Stop the constant pain caused by this condition and find a solution by <a href="http://www.yourwebsite.com">clicking here </a>.

Many experienced article marketers believe using phrases like "click here or "go here now" do not work well. Their argument is that it seems like you are overselling the product. From my own personal experience, I have found including these phrases and attaching the affiliate link to them actually does work. Again, this is something you can try on your own to see what works best for you. However, keep in mind, your resource box absolutely must contain your keyword phrase with a link. This is essential for gaining a better page rank on Google.

An example of a resource box that is useless and will not get your reader to buy your product is one like this:

Joe Blow is a professional coach that has been in the business since 1992. He has dealt with this sort of problem for nearly 20 years and knows all about how to get results. To find see what he recommends go to: www.blahblahblah.com.

No one cares who Joe Blow is. People want solutions to their problems and usually don't care who it is that is going to give it to them. If you write a good article and follow it with a good resource box, they won't care who you are. They just want the solution to their problem!

I also recommend not filling out the author bio section (sites like Ezine Articles provides these) with traditional bio information. Providing a bio gives the reader another reason to click off of your article and read something that will take their mind off of what they just read.

Instead, use the bio box to speak to the reader's problem. In the article about yeast infections, for example, include something such as: *Yeast infections are embarrassing, you don't have to deal with them any longer.*

I don't fill out who the "author" is or their history. This may be necessary for things like weight loss or selling "how to make money online" products, but not for problem solving. I've tested this so I'm not just pulling it out of nowhere. During the test, the one without a bio got 11 more sales than the one that did. And I ran the test for a month.

Something to keep in mind:
The link you include in your resource box does not necessarily have to be the one that takes the reader to the product page. You do have the option of creating your own pre-sales page (a page that tells the reader more about the product and then directs them to the product page). Some marketers believe having a pre-sales page helps generate more sales.

Also, you can direct the reader to what is known as a "squeeze page." This is a Web page that asks the reader to enter their email address to receive more information. Ideally, you will want to create a squeeze page to build an e-mail list. When it comes to sales, people who put their faith in you with one purchase will most likely buy from you again. Being able to communicate with people via email on a regular basis can generate a great deal of profits. You will learn more about how to do this in Part Three.

For now, as you are just getting started in article marketing, keep things simple. Let your article pre-sell the product and send them directly to the product sales page.

CHAPTER THREE: Finding Readers (Who Will Become Buyers) For Your Articles

Now that the writing part is done, it's time to start submitting your articles to article directories. In this section, we will focus on the most popular of them all, Ezine Articles (ezinearticles.com).

Please keep in mind, Ezine Article's article approval times can vary greatly. For this reason, it's best if you stay consistent and do submissions every day so you will constantly have traffic going through your affiliate link.

If you can afford the Premium Membership Ezine Articles offers, it's well worth it. Your articles will get approved in about an hour. Now this may not seem like much, but when you're waiting a week to get an article approved, it can be very frustrating and it slows down your moneymaking efforts. You can also schedule the times you want your articles to come out.

In regard to maximizing the traffic from the Ezine Articles Web site itself, your goal is to have your article appear on the "Recently Published" list on the site. Ezine Articles stops approving articles each weekday at 6 p.m. As a premium member, you can schedule your article to appear after 6PM. If you do this, your article will be stay on the "Recently Published" list until the morning because, at that time, your only competition would be with the few other people who might be using the same scheduling strategy. Doing this will increase the traffic to your site. More traffic = more sales!

In fact, you could schedule 10 articles to be released at the same time and dominate the "Recently Published" list.

While I want you to only invest as little money as possible to begin with, do consider investing in the premium membership. Over time, it will end up paying for itself.

Start by submitting three articles per day for your chosen niche. Once you get a few of your articles ranked in the first few search pages of Google, you can lessen the amount of articles you are submitting for one niche and begin to work on a new one.

Once you have articles submitted, it's time to work on a technique known as "backlinking."

Backlinking

The most powerful way to get traffic to your articles is if they are listed on the first three search pages of Google when someone types in your keyword or keyword phrase. Posting your article on Ezine Articles or any other article directory will go along way to help get your article ranked high on Google, but there is more work to be done to have it reach as high as it can … and stay ranked high.

To keep your article doing well on Google, you have to leave the link to your article on as many established, already high-ranking sites as possible. This is known as "backlinking."

The Ezine Articles Web site has a lot of content, is updated frequently, and gets a lot of traffic. Because of this, Google loves Ezine Articles and ranks the content found on the site very high. Many times an article appearing on Ezine Articles will hold one of the top slots on the front page of Google for your keyword for a day or two after it is indexed. Unfortunately, it's not going to stay there. You are going to have to get some backlinking going on to make it stay.

If you picked your keywords correctly, you will have no problem getting your article ranking well in a short amount of time. Obviously, the more competition you're up against the longer it will take. One thing about competition: If you're willing to outwork them you can take their rank away from them.

Google likes it when your links are coming from relevant content and popular Web sites. Your next goal is to create relevant content and link all your articles together.

Here's how you do that.

Take one of the original articles you wrote. Look over the article and determine how you can rewrite it. You don't have to start from the blank page again. Simply reword and rework what you have already written.

Once you have done this once, try it again, preferably four to five times per article.

In the article-marketing world, rewriting articles is calling "spinning." There are many software programs out there you can purchase which will automatically spin your articles many times over thus saving you hours of work.

However, when you first start out, try rewriting an article yourself. Even when you write the original article, be flexible while you keep in mind that you will be rewriting the content.

Although using software can save you some time, often, after an article has been spun, it comes out not making any sense. The sentences are rearranged and the words are jumbled. While the overall theme of the article is kept in tact, it's not necessarily going to be an article a reader would finish reading. On the one hand, if your sole purpose is to use the article for backlinking to help your Google rank, whether or not a reader finds the article of value really doesn't matter. On the other hand, you will need to decide how you feel about posting low-quality content and whether it is something you feel comfortable with.

The good news is, while the quality of your articles may be important, unique content is not. Each one of your articles does not have to be on a new topic. As mentioned above, you can reword, rewrite and even rearrange the same article to create new content.

The bottom line is that article marketing has a lot to do with numbers. The fact is, the more content you have out in different places, the more chances you have to make a sale. Do you really think the Internet is so small that the same person that read your first article at Ezine Articles is going to then see your Squidoo lens, other articles, Hubpages – and anywhere else you post some spun content – is going to realize it is duplicate content?

Not likely. But there is a good chance that 1,000 different people may see one of your articles on one of these sites because you have so much content out there and so many opportunities for people to come across it.

Once you have your main article rewritten a few times, it is now time to create something called a "content funnel."

As mentioned before, the goal is to have your article ranked as high on the pages of Google as possible. The more links pointing to your article the better your chances of ranking high.

Your content funnel might look something like this:

- Your main article is posted on the Ezine Articles Web site.
- Rewrite #1 of the article is posted on another article directory.
- Rewrite #2 of the article is posted on Hubpages.com.
- Rewrite #3 of the article is posted on Blogspot.com.

The best sites to post your articles on are the heavily visited Web 2.0 sites such as Weebly.com, LiveJournal.com or Squidoo.com. Start out with 4 to 5 of the hundreds of Web 2.0 sites that exist and put one version of your rewritten article on each one of them.

Within each article there needs to be two links. One link will point back to your main article (the one posted on EzineArticles.com) and the second link will point to one of your other article rewrites.

Here is what an excerpt of an article with links would look like:

One of the first rules of <u>leash training your dog</u> is to first get your puppy use to the leash. A dog never exposed to a leash before might be shocked and scared there is something hanging off his neck that restricts his movements. Try a few days just letting the leash trail behind him or go for very short 'walks' on a long loose leash, always ending in a positive note. Don't just throw it on and start with 'heel' on the first day. This can be overwhelming to a lot of puppies.

Some young dogs, especially the more stubborn ones, won't appreciate being led around by the neck. If he starts to really fight the leash, just let the leash stay slack in your hands until he is done. Do not try to pull on it or let it go. The former will make him more afraid and fight more, and the latter will make it seem like if he just fights you he will get his way.

Start your <u>dog training</u> with a fun calling exercise; use your puppy's name or whatever you think will make him come to you. Then as he comes forward, simply pick up the slack in the leash. Praise the puppy with hugs or treats and he will eventually learn that by following you good things happen.

In this example, you would place a link within the keywords of the niche you have chosen. (In this example they are "leash training your dog" and "dog training.") In an article, words that contain links are known as "anchor text."

The "leash training your dog" link would point to your EzineArticles.com article. The "dog training" link would point to, as an example, the rewritten article you posted on LiveJournal.com (or whatever other site where you posted another one of your rewrites).

Make sure you vary the anchor text you use. You don't want all your articles having the exact anchor text because that would look unnatural. If your keyword is "leash training your dog," vary that anchor text to say things like "leash training your poodle" or "leash training puppies" in every other article or so.

Once you have done this, you have a content funnel with links all pointing to the article you are trying to rank high in Google. Relevant content all linking together and to your main article equals lots of link juice!!

Creating a content funnel can be as basic or as intricate as you would like it to be, depending on how much time you want to devote to doing so. After you have posted your first batch of articles, you may want to create a second funnel that looks something like this:

- Rewrite #4 of your article is posted on Scribd.com. It contains a link to article #3, which was posted on Blogspot.com.
- Rewrite #5 of your article is posted on GoArticles.com and also links to article #3 and #4.
- Rewrite #6 is posted on your own blog and again, links to article #3 and also #5.

With this content funnel, rather than linking directly to your main article (which is still at EzineArticles.com), you are focusing on convincing Google your Blogspot.com article is an important one which other, popular Web sites are linking to. More traffic to your Blogpost.com post means more traffic to your main article.

Now, this does take time to do, but it also helps you boost your search engine rankings quite dramatically. There is no end to this either. You can build out as much as you want as far as funnels go. Couple this with the other methods I'm about to show you, and you'll be kicking ass as far as how high your articles are ranking.

Don't forget that you can blast out these spun versions of articles to the other directories as well. Put one link pointing to the article you want to rank for (or landing page) and another link to one of the Web 2.0 sites you have built. Many times you'll be surprised that not only will you have your article ranking on the front page, but you'll also get some of these Web 2.0 properties listed up there.

As with article rewriting, there are software programs out there (such as one called Senuke), which automate back-linking and save you a great deal of time.

Once you have all of your articles posted, there are other, simple things you can do to give them a boost.

The first is to "ping" each site on which you posted your article. To "ping" means you are letting various Web sites know your site has new content. Use a site such as Pingomatic.com to post the link of each of your articles.

You also want to "social bookmark" the articles posted on Web 2.0 sites. This submits the link to your Web 2.0-site content to other Web 2.0 sites. Use a site like Socialmarker.com to submit to a long list of sites. (It's also a great site to get ideas for other sites to post your articles on.)

Finally, on each site to which you post an article, your Web page will come with an RSS feed. You will want to take each RSS feed, along with the RSS feed you are given from EzineArticles.com, and submit it to RSS directories. Visit RSSFeedMachine.com to find a list of RSS directories to submit to.

CHAPTER FOUR: Other Ways To Get Traffic...And Sales

Your Own Blog

Another way to generate more traffic and more sales is by posting your articles on your own blog on Web site.

These days, setting up a Web site and a blog could not be easier.

First, purchase a domain name that contains the keyword or phrase of the niche you have chosen.

Next, sign up for Web hosting with a reputable company, such as Hostgator.com

Once you have your Web hosting account set up, create a WordPress blog on your Web site. These days, WordPress is the most popular blogging platform on the Web. While I won't go into detail on how to set up your domain, Web site and blog within this book, please be reassured doing so is very easy. Web hosts such as Hostgator have video tutorials and customer service people who will help you get set up.

Once you have your Web site and WordPress blog set up, take each one of your articles and post them on the blog. Unlike the articles you posted on other sites, the articles on your blog will have your affiliate link within them.

No, you won't be using your blog to link back to your other articles with this. But trust me, having a blog with direct links to the product you are promoting will bring you extra money.

If you post articles on your blog consistently, you will get a good page rank on Google and it will happen quickly. Think about it; if you post just two articles a day, at the end of the 30 days you will have 60 posts on your blog. Keep doing it and in three months you'll have 180. The more you prove to Google your site is a reliable site for good content that is updated often, you will rank high for your chosen keywords.

Something to keep in mind: Besides having another avenue for potential sales, an important reason for having your own blog hosted on your own site is because *no one* can take it away from you. The Web can be unpredictable. You could spend months building links to an article you have posted on another site only to wake up one day to discover that site has been shut down. All of your hard work will have been lost. If you have your own site, you will always have your articles and links posted on a site you can rely on.

Posting On Other Article Directories

Earlier in the book, you were instructed to post your articles on Web 2.0 sites. The other sites you must post on are other article directories. While EzineArticles.com is the biggest, there are still many others you need to have your articles on. Here are just a few:

- GoArticles.com
- ArticleDashboard.com

- ArticlesBase.com
- SearchWarp.com
- Buzzle.com

Making Videos and Podcasts Out of Articles

To get ahead of your competition, you may want to create videos or podcasts out of your articles. Because your articles are so short, creating a 3- to 5-minute video to place on all the popular video sites (including YouTube) would take mere minutes. Simply record yourself reading the article and combine the audio with a few photos. When you post the video, you can place a link to your main article to help with backlinking, or place your affiliate link taking the viewer right to the product you are promoting. Experiment with this to see what results work best for you.

You can then take the same audio you used for the video and create short podcasts. Post the podcasts on ITunes and other podcast directories.

Just like the articles you posted, you can submit your videos to social bookmarking sites and submit the RSS feed to RSS directories to get even more backlinks.

Leaving Comments On Other People's Blogs

While creating lots of backlinks is a good thing, what helps the most is getting *quality* backlinks. One way to do this is by leaving a link to your main article within a comment on a blog. While this will help you tremendously, it's not the easiest thing to accomplish.

Many article marketers know about the value blog commenting, but what often happens is that when you when you leave a comment on a blog and put a link in your comment, it gets deleted as spam. However, there is a way around it.

There is something called "Keyword luv" which is a plug-in that allows blog commenters to create hyperlinks to their sites within their blog comment without pissing off the blog owners. Blog owners know you're going to try and get links to your site, so they just made it easier for you.

Do a Google search and type in "blogs that use Keywordluv." Once you find a blog that will allow you to leave your link, be respectful of the blog owner by reading the blog post and then leaving a good comment containing a link to your article.

Also, keep in mind, when leaving a link it must contain anchor text. You cannot leave a link that looks like this:

http://www.linktomyarticle.com

It must look like this:

Learn How To Leash Train Your Dog

(As you learned earlier, use your keywords as your anchor text and place your link within those words.)

You can find more blogs to comment on by searching for "do-follow" blogs.

Also, go to Google Images and do a search for the following files:

ifollowblue.gif
ifollowgreen.gif
ifollowpink.gif
ifollowpurple.gif
ifollowltgreen.gif
ifolloworange.gif
ifollowwhite.gif
ifollowmagenta.gif
ifollow.gif
utrackback_ifollow.gif
ifollow-red.png

If you find a site that has this graphic on it, it will be a blog that will allow you to leave a link.

Yahoo Answers and Forums

Another popular site is Yahoo Answers. Not only will you find ideas for future articles here, but also there are countless opportunities for you to leave a link to your article.

Do a search in the category of your chosen niche. Find questions which you can give answers to. Within your answer, include the link to your article.

Forums (also known as "message boards") are also great places to leave your links. People come to a message board to ask for advice and seek support for their problem. Create your own account and include a link to your article within your profile signature (again, using anchor text).

Join in on the conversation. Not only will participating on forums help with backlinking and Google rank, but people reading your forum posts will get curious, click on your link and check out your article.

Twitter

At the time this book was written, Twitter has become one of the most popular sites on the Web. No doubt, in a few years time, another site will have eclipsed it. But for now, Twitter is still an excellent tool for your article marketing endeavors.

Creating a Twitter account and begin to follow many people. If your niche is, an example, dog training, do a Google search for dog trainers who are on Twitter. Look at the people who are following the person you found. Follow those people. You want to find people on Twitter who have an interest in your niche. You may also want to check out sites such as WeFollow.com to find people active in your chosen niche.

Once you begin to follow people, most people will follow your back. Once your followers list has grown to hundreds, or even thousands, begin posting links to your articles. Within a post, write something casual, but attention-grabbing such as:

You won't believe what they're teaching people when it comes to leash training your dog. Check out this article (link to article).

You don't want to bombard your followers with links (or

they will un-follow you). Be subtle when it comes to posting your links.

Get Creative

There are a ton of ways you can get even more traffic to your articles if you're willing to think outside the box a little bit. These are just a few ways that will make you quite successful if you're willing to put the time in.

Remember, there is no easy path to success online. If there were, everybody would be doing it. It takes work and dedication, but if you're willing to put forth the effort, the success will come.

Don't Give Up!

Do not be afraid to fail!

Some niches that you pick just are not going to sell very well and some sites you post on just won't get traffic. It's just the nature of the beast. It's ok if you are testing and write articles for two weeks and never get a sale.

If that happens to you, don't give up! Just pick another niche and test it out. The only way you will fail is if you give up and stop trying.

CHAPTER FIVE: Outsourcing To Make Your Life Easier And Build Your Online Empire Faster

Let me show you how to scale this stuff up and start putting some serious money in your pocket by the use of outsourcing.

All the article-marketing techniques I have given you within this book are easy implement once you get the hang of it. In fact, as you have probably noticed, article marketing takes very little money to get started. At the minimum, all you need is to spend less then $10 on a domain name you will use to forward your affiliate link to.

The truth is, what article marketing does take is a great deal of time.

The key to successful article marketing is budgeting your time the best way you can. Let's say you spend three hours a day writing six articles. Now, let's say that one of those articles earns you a sale of $26. You made $26 for three hours of effort, which works out to a little less than $8.50 per hour.

But what if you took part of that $26 and hired someone to rewrite those six articles? It is possible to hire someone to rewrite articles for as little as $2/article.

If you were to hire someone, you have just spent $12, have a batch of new articles to post and still have a profit of $14. Most importantly, you saved yourself the hours it would have taken to either re-write your articles or write new ones.

What do you do with your free time? Start writing in another niche! Get a few articles out and repeat the process again. Make some money and then pay someone to rewrite them for you freeing up *more* of your time.

But wait, you still have $14 left over from the $26 you earned. You would be wise to invest it into outsourcing and pay someone to do your social bookmarking and submitting your RSS feed to directories. Again, it is possible to hire a person who will do this sort of work for $2-3/hour.

There are three different places that you can go to get people to do most of these tasks for you. They are Odesk.com, Digitalpoint.com and Wickedfire.com.

On these three sites you can find people who will do all the social bookmarking, article writing, article rewriting and RSS submissions you will need. You can find people to do these for a one-time fee or you can pay by the hour.

It is absolutely important to do these tasks yourself for the very first time before you hire someone to do them for you. This way you get a true understanding of how to do them. If you do these tasks yourself first, you will know how to make sure it is done right when you hire someone to do them for you.

Don't be afraid that hiring people to do these tasks will cut into your profits. It won't. It will actually multiply them! While you are paying a very small sum for people to do all the "grunt work" that is so time consuming, you are off getting researching new niches and coming up with more ideas to make more money from.

Here is a small breakdown of what I pay for services:

I write all my articles myself. I do not trust someone to write decent articles for me. I know good writers are out there, but to get a good one you are going to pay at least $5 for a 250-word article. Truth be told, you never know how good they really are until you see their work. By the time you see it, you've already paid for it. If your goal is to submit three articles per day and you hire a writer to supply you with enough articles to submit for one week, you will be paying $105 for articles you're not guaranteed are of good quality. To me, that's more money than I care to spend.

Now, your experience might be different. If you find an exceptional writer, start off by hiring them to do 3 to 5 articles. If you are happy with their writing, by all means, have them write all your articles.

What I do is pay someone $1.67 per hour to rewrite articles I have written. On a typical day, I will send five articles to be rewritten. I have the writer create three rewrites of the original article. It usually takes the writer about two hours. For $3.34 I now have 15 new articles to post.

I also hire someone to submit all my articles to the various directories. It usually takes them about an hour to do it. I pay $1.11/hour.

I then pay someone $1.11/hour to do social bookmarking and RSS submissions.

Finally, I pay someone to do nothing but build links to my

sites through bookmarking, blog commenting, directory submissions and various other ways. I pay $3.50/hour.

All total, I pay about $85 per week for these services. The time they save me is priceless. Thanks to outsourcing, I regularly make enough in one day to pay for the whole week.

At the beginning, it is important for you to learn how to this on your own. But after awhile you are only holding yourself back if you do not utilize outsourcing. As an article marketer, your main priority is to find money-making products and come up with ways to promote them. You do not need to spend your time doing tedious tasks.

If, for whatever reason, you don't feel comfortable out-sourcing this work to other people, invest in software that will automate a lot of these tasks (such as Senuke).

PART ONE CONCLUSION: It All Comes Down To This...

1. Figure out a niche you want to promote.

2. Look for a product within that niche you want to promote.

3. Acquire an affiliate link for the product you have chosen.

4. Buy a domain name and have it forward to your affiliate link.

5. Find the keywords that you will be using.

6. Write your articles around your keywords. Follow the guidelines for writing them.

7. Rewrite your articles.

8. Build your content funnel.

9. Social bookmark your sites, ping them and submit their RSS feeds.

10. Back link your content funnel with blog commenting. Find blogs you can comment on by doing a Google search using the terms: "keyword luv" and "dofollow blogs."

11. Build your own blog and post your original articles on a regular basis.

12. Utilize Yahoo Answers, Twitter, YouTube and other technique you can think of.

13. MAKE MONEY!

PART TWO: Your 30-Day Online Money-Making Plan Of Action

This step-by-step process that I'm about to show you was designed to take you about 2 to 3 hours per day. At first, it may take you a little longer, but as you get comfortable doing the steps you will find your speed will increase.

If you cannot get through the steps each day, do not get upset and quit because you are behind! Just keep at it and do as much as you can. Pick up where you left off the next day if you get a little behind. Just keep working and you will get results.

Every day there will be a list of tasks to do for the day. Follow the list and you will do fine. Each day there is a "done" box for you to check off your tasks as you finish them. This way it will be very easy to keep track of what you did for the day.

Realize that this process is completely repeatable. Even if you are making $20/day, that is great! All you have to do is repeat this exact same process, but this time you'll do it with another niche. And if that second niche makes you $20/day as well, then now you're up to $40/day.

Learning how to do these fundamental Internet marketing tasks yourself is the beginning of a learning process that will give you the education and understanding you will need to make your article marketing business succeed.

ALWAYS REMEMBER:

The Internet is *constantly* changing. You may use one method to drive traffic to your site (and have great success with it) only to wake up one morning to discover a Web site has changed its rules and you can no longer use your current method. Also, new Web sites pop up every day. Some of them become extremely popular very quickly and you need to know about them and create an account on them. Always be doing research and keeping yourself up to date on what is changing and what sites are getting the most traffic. As the Web changes, change right along with it to ensure you continue making money.

Day 1

Today you are going to decide what product you are going to promote.

Go to Clickbank.com and search through the Marketplace to find a digital product you feel comfortable promoting, that pays a good affiliate commission, and that you see is already selling well. While Clickbank is not the only site to find products to promote, it is one of the few sites that gives precise information on what products are selling and how well they are selling.

There are a few things you are going to want to look at while searching for a product to promote.

First look at the "gravity" of the product. This number will tell you how many people were paid that week for selling that particular product. If the number is above 75 then you know the product sells well. If you see a product that has a gravity of 500, then you know it selling extremely well. Some article marketing experts choose products that have a gravity of 20 to 50 because this indicates that, while the product is selling, you will not have as much competition with other Internet marketers when it comes to promoting it. Whether you choose a high-selling product with a high gravity or one with a low gravity is up to you. Think about the niche you have chosen and the problem you are solving. Choose the best product for your needs.

I would advise that you stay away from promoting "How to Make Money Online" products as well as weight loss-related products. Both of those niches are extremely flooded by others marketing those products. Making some sales in these niches isn't impossible, but getting consistent sales with these can be difficult.

Recently, the relationship niche (how to get your ex back, dating, catch a cheating spouse) has become very over-crowded with competition as well. If you decide you want to try any of the making-money niches (this includes forex trading), weight loss or dating niches, go ahead, just know you're up against a lot of Internet marketers vying for po-tential sales.

After you have decided on a product there are two sites to check to see how much it is in demand – or not in demand.

First, go to EzineArticles.com. At the top of the page, you will see a search box. Within that search box type in the name of the product you have chosen followed by the word "review." Click on the "Search" button to begin. Once the page comes up, scroll to the very bottom where you will see a list of "Recently published articles," "Most viewed articles for the last 90 days," and "Most published articles for the last 90 days."

Look through the "Most viewed articles for the last 90 days" to see how many views each one has had. If you see articles that have gotten 3,000 or more views, it's a pretty good bet there are lots of people interested in that topic. Click on the link to the article that has the most views. Bookmark this page. You are going to come back to it to-morrow.

Next, go to Yahoo Answers and search for questions that your product could solve. As an example, if you're niche was "how to stop hair loss for women" do a search for "best way a woman can stop hair loss."

If you see there are a lot of questions pertaining to the problem your product could solve, this is a good indication that you have probably picked a good product.

Now, begin looking at the answers people are leaving for these questions. Are those people leaving links to products in their answers? If they all are, then you know the competition is going to be stiff at Yahoo Answers. If there are no links to products in the answers, you may have good success making sales just by leaving a link in your answers.

Picking a product and doing research will probably take you a few hours. Take your time! Picking good products is vital to success. If you hurry through this and select a garbage product, you will not do as well as you could have with a good product.

That's it for Day 1.Tomorrow you will move on to keyword research.

Day 2

Today, you are going to concentrate on keyword research. More specifically, you are going to look for something called "long-tail" keywords.

Long-tail keywords are phrases (three words or longer), people type into the search engines when looking for something.

Many years ago, there was a time when, as an article marketer, you could have chosen basic keywords such as "weight loss" or "dog training" or "hair loss" and created a content funnel around them. These days, you have far too much competition with these keywords and, now, you have to dig in to find much more specified keyword phrases (or "long-tail" keywords). While "weight loss" is out of your reach "postnatal weight loss" may not be.

For this example, we will look at the relationship niche.

Remember that article you bookmarked yesterday? Go back to it.

In your browser, click on the "View" menu. (It can be found at the top, on the left, next to "File" and "Edit.") Scroll down and choose "Source." A window will pop up in your text editor. There you will see a lot of writing and symbols. This is the Web page's HTML code. It will look something like this:

meta http-equiv="Content-Type" content="text/html; charset=ISO-8859-1">

<meta http-equiv="Content-Language" content="en-us">
<meta name="description" content="How to Get Your Ex Back - The Simple Guide">
<meta name="**keywords**" content="get ex back, win back ex, get ex girlfriend back, get ex boyfriend back, break up, breakup">

Look for the keywords. In this example, they are:

- get ex back
- win back ex
- get ex girlfriend back
- get ex boyfriend back
- break up
- breakup

Open your favorite text editor and create a new file for all the details for this project. Copy these keywords into this new file for safekeeping. You are going to be looking through this list to come up with the long-tail keywords you will choose to use.

Like you did yesterday, do another search for your product name and the word "review." Yesterday, when you did this exercise, you bookmarked the one that had been read the most. Today, you are going to look through the other articles on the "Most viewed" list and do exactly the same—look at the keywords, copy them and paste them into your keyword file.

Once you have a few dozen long-tailed keywords via EzineArticels.com, it's time to get more from another source. There are many keyword tools that you can use.

Everyone has his/her own favorite. It will be up to you to find one that you like the best. For now, try the free version of WordTracker.com or the Google Adwords Keyword Tool.

By typing the keywords you found into these research tools, you will be able to see an approximate daily search average for the phrase you entered.

Also, don't totally rely on the keywords you have found. Use your own imagination to come up with variations of the phrases. With the relationship niche, examples of variations might be:

- get my ex back
- getting an ex back
- ways to get an ex back

Any phrase you see that has at least 30 searches a day needs to be saved. Open a new file to save these phrases. You will no doubt be using some of them.

Once you have 10 to 20 of these long-tailed keywords that have more than 30 searches/day, it's time to check out the competition.
To check competition, go to Google and type one of your long-tailed keyword phrases into the search box. When Google brings you back the results, you will want to look at *everything* on the first page.

Take note of the number of result pages it brings back.

Then, look for any free sites such as YouTube, Ezine

Articles, Scribd, Hubpage, WordPress, Blogger or any other page that is a free source that shows up on the first page of search results. If you see these sites, this is a good indication you can compete with this keyword phrase.

However, if see nothing but authority sites such as Amazon, Wikipedia, iVillage.com or MSNBC.com, it would probably be a good idea to leave that keyword alone. That's not saying that you cannot get on the first page eventually, but for the time being, you need to focus on easier challenges.

Next, do your Google search again, this time putting quotation marks around the keyword and then hit the search button. Once the results come up, pay attention to the number of results you receive. If that number is under 20,000, you will have a good chance to rank for that keyword.

The last thing you want to check for is any paid ads which appear on the results page. If there are more than three paid ads and the number of results is under 20,000, you have yourself a winner.

Go through your entire list of long-tail keywords and do the same Google searches. Make sure to keep all the phrases you discover and add them to your file.

That's it for Day 2.

Day 3

Today, you are going to sign up for all the sites you will be using for this project.

You will need an email address. I highly recommend creating a new GMail account to be used specifically for signing up for Web sites.

While using the same username and password for each site might be the most secure option, it will make it very easy to sign in when you're ready to use them. Remember to save your username and password to these sites to the text file you saved for this project.

Go ahead and sign up for the sites below:

- Squidoo.com
- Blogger.com
- WordPress.com
- Hubpages.com
- SocialMarker.com (Only sign up for the "best" and "do-follow" lists on this site.)
- EzineArticles.com (Create two separate accounts at EzineArticles.com.)
- GoArticles.com
- ArticlesBase.com
- ArticlesFactory.com
- ArticleAlley.com
- ArticleBiz.com
- EasyArticles.com
- Amazines.com

- ArticleCube.com
- SearchWarp.com
- ArticleDashboard.com
- Buzzle.com
- YahooAnswers.com
- RSSFeedMachine.com (Sign up for the RSS directories listed on this site.)

Day 4

Today, go to EzineArticles.com and read every article you can find that has been written about your niche. Follow the links in the resource boxes and see what sort of pages the article's author is sending the reader to.

Are the links in the resource boxes going to a Web site, a blog, Hubpages.com, a Squidoo lens or directly to the product page? Most people will have two links in their resource box. Make sure you check them *both* to see where they are going. Read the pages those links have taken you to and note how they are worded. Would they make you want to click on the link to buy the product? Ask yourself why or why not.

Go to Squidoo, WordPress, Hubpages and Blogger. Notice how the top-ranking pages look. What type of pictures do they have on them? Look at their titles. Where are the links placed on these pages? Do they have banner ads? What are they doing that caught *your* eye?

Take notes as to what other Internet marketers are doing to give them the best chance of success. You will want to implement these things on your own sites. Compare the most highly ranked pages to ones that are not ranked as high. Try to figure out what the reason or difference is. Is it keyword optimization or content?

That is it for Day 4.

Day 5

Today, and during the days to come, there will be a list of numbered tasks. Just follow the tasks in their order. At the end of each task there will be a box following the word "Done." Each time you finish a task, check it off as "Done." This way, if you do not finish everything for the day, you know where you left off. Organization is crucial to your success as well as following through on these tasks. If you do a half-assed job, you can expect half-assed results.

Let's get to work!

1. Write three articles around one of the keywords you have chosen to use. Submit these articles to Ezine Articles. Make sure your keyword is included in the title, first paragraph, somewhere in the middle of your article, and in the resource box. Be sure your resource box has a strong call to action. You have to write it in a way that will make people want to click on your link.

Make the resource box an extension of your article. Think of it as being like the last paragraph of the article in which you invite the reader to go further with you for more information. Doing this will make your click-through rates much greater.

Don't forget to include your keyword in the anchor text of the links you place in your resource box.

Submit the articles to be approved. Because you have just created a new account, approval will take longer.

DONE ❑

2. Go to the Blogger account you created and post your articles there along with your links.

DONE ❏

3. Go to Google and add your Blogger page URL (google.com/addurl).

DONE ❏

4. Go to Bing.com and add your Blogger page URL (bing.com/docs/submit.aspx).

DONE ❏

5. Go to Pingomatic.com and ping your Blogger URL and RSS Feed.

DONE ❏

6. Social bookmark your Blogger page at the social bookmark sites you signed up for at SocialMarker.com.

DONE ❏

7. Answer four questions at Yahoo Answers, and put a link to your Blogger page in two of the four answers.

DONE ❏

Day 6

1. Write three articles around your keywords and submit them to Ezine Articles.

DONE ❏

2. Submit your Blogger blog's RSS Feed to the RSS aggregators found at RSSFeedMachine.com.

DONE ❏

3. Answer four questions at Yahoo Answers, leaving links in two of the answers.

DONE ❏

Day 7

1. Write three articles and submit them to your second account at Ezine Articles. Two accounts with EzineArticles.com is necessary because the site only allows you to submit 10 articles before they review your status.

After their review, they will either choose to upgrade your account and allow you to submit as many articles as you would like, or make you submit an extra 25 articles before upgrading you to Platinum status.

Because we are going to be writing three articles each day, there would be a hold up on submitting any more articles once you reach 10. By opening two accounts you will be able to submit 20 articles before reaching a pause in submission.

By then, you should have had one of your accounts upgraded. Also, because you are not a Platinum author yet, nor are you paying for an account upgrade, it will sometimes take a few days to get your articles approved. This way you will have two accounts that have their days staggered and you will have articles going live
day after day.   DONE ❏

2. Go to Squidoo and Hubpages and build one page on each site. Again, go back to your notes and build your pages around the elements that made the high-ranking pages you checked out on Day 4 so successful. Remember to build these pages around your keywords.

Make sure your keywords are in the title, in the text, and in anchor text when you put your links in. Make three modules in each page. (You'll see what a "module" is once you are at the site.)

On your Squidoo page, put a link in the first module to your Hubpage. The second module needs to be linked to your Blogger page. The link in the third module will be to the domain that is forwarding your affiliate link.

Do the same thing at your Hubpage. Link the first module to your Squidoo lens and do the others as you have instructed above. Make sure to save the URLs of your Squidoo and Hubpage and their RSS feeds to the text file you are keeping for this project.

DONE ❏

3. Add the URL for your Squidoo and Hubpage to Google URL (google.com/addurl) and Bing.com (bing.com/docs/submit.aspx).

DONE ❏

4. Answer four questions at Yahoo Answers. Leave links in two of the four of the answers .

DONE ❏

DAY 8

1. Write three articles and submit them to Ezine Articles.

DONE ❏

2. Take the RSS feeds for your Squidoo and Hubpage and submit them to RSS directories found on RSSFeedMachine.com.

DONE ❏

3. Social bookmark your Squidoo and Hubpage to the social bookmarking sites using SocialMarker.com.

DONE ❏

4. Answer four questions at Yahoo Answers. Leave links in two answers.

DONE ❏

Day 9

Your first articles from Ezine Articles should go live today (if they did not yesterday). You should see a small burst of traffic from them to the Web site of the product you are promoting. Be sure to log into Clickbank to check your click-through rate to see how many people actually followed the link in your resource box. (You can find these stats by clicking on the "Reports" tab.) You want to have a click-through rate of at least 25 percent. Higher is always better, and lower will sometimes happen, but you should shoot for around 25 percent. If, after awhile, you are not getting close to that number of click-throughs, you either need to reword your resource box or write a more compelling article.

To determine the percent of your click-through rate, first look at the number of views your article received, then look at the number of clicks your affiliate link received. Do some quick math to see what percentage of those article visitors checked out the product page.

1. Write three articles around your keyword and submit them to Ezine Articles.

DONE ❏

2. Rewrite the three articles that went live and go to WordPress.com. You are going to use the articles you just rewrote to start a blog. In each post, make sure your keywords are in the right places, including the anchor text for the link you are including.

As a note, WordPress.com is a free service, like Blogger, which allows anyone to set up a blog within minutes (hosted on the WordPress.com site). Do not confuse it with WordPress.org, which is the site for people who want to host their own blog on their own site using the WordPress software. If you want to do the latter, go to WordPress.org to download the software and learn how to use it.

DONE ❏

3. Submit your WordPress blog's URL to Google URL (google.com/addurl) and Bing.com (bing.com/docs/submit.aspx).

DONE ❏

4. Ping your WordPress blog at Pingomatic.com.

DONE ❏

5. Answer four questions at Yahoo Answers, leaving links in two of the four answers.

DONE ❏

Day 10

Your second set of articles should go live today. Remember to check your click-through stats to see how your resource box is converting.

1. Write three articles around your keywords and submit them to Ezine Articles.

DONE ❏

2. Go back to your Squidoo and Hubpage. Create a new module. In that module, put a link to the WordPress blog you created yesterday.

DONE ❏

3. Ping your Squidoo and Hubpage URL and RSS feeds at Pingomatic.com.

DONE ❏

4. Social bookmark the posts from your WordPress blog you created.

DONE ❏

5. Answer four questions at Yahoo Answers, leaving links in two of the four answers.

DONE ❏

Day 11

1. Write three articles around your keywords and submit them to Ezine Articles.

DONE ❏

2. Take the first three articles that were approved and submit them to the article sites you signed up for on Day 3.

DONE ❏

3. Go back to Squidoo and Hubpage. Add three RSS modules. Put your RSS feed to your Ezine Articles author page in one, your RSS feed to your Hubpage/Squidoo page (depending on which one you are on) on the other, and the RSS feed to your WordPress.com blog on the third.

DONE ❏

4. Ping the URL's for your Squidoo and Hubpage at Pingomatic.com.

DONE ❏

5. Answer four questions at Yahoo Answers, leaving links in two of the four answers.

DONE ❏

Day 12

1. Write three articles around your keywords and submit them to Ezine Articles.

DONE ❑

2. Take your second set of approved articles and rewrite them.

DONE ❑

3. Go to your WordPress blog and make posts out of the three articles you just rewrote.

DONE ❑

4. Ping your WordPress blog URL at Pingomatic.com.

DONE ❑

5. Answer four questions at Yahoo Answers, leaving links in three of the answers.

DONE ❑

Day 13

1. Write three articles around your keywords and submit them to Ezine Articles.

DONE ❑

2. Social bookmark your new posts on your WordPress blog to the sites you signed up for on Day 3.

DONE ❑

3. Social bookmark some of your articles from Ezine Articles, as well as some that you had submitted to the other article directories, to the sites you signed up for on Day 3.

DONE ❑

4. Submit your Ezine Author RSS feed to the RSS aggregators found at RSSFeedMachine.com.

DONE ❑

5. Answer four questions at Yahoo Answers, leaving links in three answers.

DONE ❑

6. Visit Clickbank.com to check out your click-through rates. Assess how well you are doing and make any changes (if needed) to boost your click-through rate.

DONE ❑

Day 14

1. Write three articles around your keywords and submit them to Ezine Articles.

DONE ❏

2. Take the second set of articles that were approved and submit them to the article directories you signed up for in Day 3.

DONE ❏

3. Go to Squidoo and Hubpages and add another module to each one. Then, go back to your Blogger page and place links to the new modules on your Blogger page. Be sure to use the right anchor text when creating links.

DONE ❏

4. Ping your URL for your Squidoo and Hubpage at Pingomatic.com

DONE ❏

5. Answer four questions at Yahoo Answers, leaving links in three answers.

DONE ❏

Day 15

You have now been putting up content for 10 solid days. It's time to do some research. It's time to check Google to find out where your pages are ranking for your keywords.

Take your keyword and, after putting it in quotations, do a Google search to see what Web pages come up

Do you have any articles that are ranking high?

Is your Squidoo or Hubpage doing well in the search engines?

Once you see how high or how low your pages are ranking, concentrate on moving them up in the search engines. How do you do that? By doing what you have been doing: building content and links.

By now you will probably have reached your limit at Ezine Articles for the number of articles they will let you submit. They will then ask you why they should allow you to become a Platinum author. You will need to send in a written reply. Here is, word for word, what I wrote. It got me approved in less than an hour.

I have submitted 10 well-researched and well-written articles. They have all been 100% unique and if given the opportunity to become a Platinum member, I will continue to submit nothing but the same high-quality content. Thank you for your time and consideration.

After you have done your research and dealt with Ezine Articles, it's time to get back to work.

1. Write three articles around keywords and submit them to Ezine Articles.

DONE ❏

2. Social bookmark articles submitted to directories *other than* Ezine Articles.

DONE ❏

3. Rewrite three articles and post them on your WordPress blog.

DONE ❏

4. Ping your WordPress blog URL at Pingomatic.com.

DONE ❏

5. Answer five questions at Yahoo Answers, leaving links in four of them.

DONE ❏

Day 16

1. Write three articles around your keywords and submit them to Ezine Articles.

DONE ❏

2. Go to Feedburner.com with your current RSS feeds and create new RSS feeds out of all the ones you have been used thus far.

DONE ❏

3. Submit the new feeds to the RSS aggregators found at RSSFeedMachine.com.

DONE ❏

4. Social bookmark yesterday's WordPress post at the sites you signed up for on SocialMarker.com.

DONE ❏

5. Answer five questions at Yahoo Answers, leaving links in four answers.

DONE ❏

Day 17

1. Write three articles around your keywords and submit them to Ezine Articles.

DONE ❏

2. Go to Squidoo and Hubpages and change up the pictures on them.

DONE ❏

3. Ping the URL for you Squidoo and Hubpage at Pingomatic.com.

DONE ❏

4. Submit recently approved articles to the article directories from Day 3.

DONE ❏

5. Answer five questions at Yahoo Answers, leaving links in four answers.

DONE ❏

Day 18

1. Write three articles around your keywords and submit them to Ezine Articles.

DONE ❏

2. Rewrite three articles and submit them as posts to your WordPress.com blog.

DONE ❏

3. Ping your WordPress blog URL at Pingomatic.com.

DONE ❏

4. Go to back to Feedburner.com to again create new RSS feeds from your current ones. Submit them to the RSS aggregators found at RSSFeedMachine.com.

DONE ❏

5. Answer five questions at Yahoo Answers, leaving links in four of the answers.

DONE ❏

Day 19

Another way to get links is via blog commenting and forum posting

Go to Google and do a search using "your keyword" (in quotations) and the word "forum" or "message board" or "blog."

Your search will bring a list of blogs you can comment on and forums you can post to.

When it comes to blog commenting, don't forget to do a "keyword luv" search as described earlier in this book. Also, when commenting, write something that directly speaks to the blog post and adds value as opposed to something general or vague. Doing so will lead to your comment being deleted. Don't forget to leave your link in anchor text for the keywords you are targeting.

Follow the same rules for forums. Put a link in the "signature" of your profile so that the link will appear in each one of your posts. Make some contributions to the forum before you even put the link in your signature.

Find forums and blogs you don't mind visiting and contributing to on a regular basis. You would be surprised by the amount of traffic you can get from forums and blogs if you represent yourself as an expert on a certain subject.

1. Write three articles around your keywords and submit them to Ezine Articles.

DONE ❑

2. Do some searching for blogs and forums you can begin commenting and posting on.

DONE ❏

3. Social bookmark yesterday's WordPress blog posts to the sites from Day 3.

DONE ❏

4. Answer five questions in Yahoo Answers, leaving links in four answers.

DONE ❏

Day 20

1. Write three articles around your keywords and submit them to Ezine Articles.

DONE ❏

2. Rewrite three articles and post them to your WordPress blog. Include links that point back to your highest-ranking article.

DONE ❏

3. Ping your WordPress Blog URL at Pingomatic.com.

DONE ❏

4. Go to your Squidoo and Hubpages and change up the pictures.

DONE ❏

5. Ping your Squidoo And Hubpage URL at Pingomatic.com.

DONE ❏

6. Answer five questions at Yahoo Answers, leaving links in four answers.

DONE ❏

Day 21

1. Write three articles around keywords and submit them to Ezine Articles.

DONE ❏

2. Add any RSS feeds to your Squidoo and Hubpages you have not yet added.

DONE ❏

3. Do some forum posting (make sure you have a link to your main article signature). Do some blog commenting.

DONE ❏

4. Take three articles that have been approved and submit them to the various article directories.

DONE ❏

5. Answer five questions at Yahoo Answers, leaving links in four answers.

DONE ❏

Day 22

1. Write three articles around your keywords and submit them to Ezine Articles.

DONE ❑

2. Go back to Blogger.com and create a new blog. Take one article that you have previously had approved and post it to this new Blogger blog. Change only the title. Keep everything else in tact just as you have it in the article at Ezine Articles. Add four RSS modules to this new blog and insert your Ezine Author RSS feed, Squidoo RSS feed, Hubpage RSS feed and WordPress.com blog RSS feed.

DONE ❑

3. Add the new Blogger URL to Google (google.com/addurl) and Bing (bing.com/docs/submit.aspx).

DONE ❑

4. Ping the new Blogger URL at Pingomatic.com.

DONE ❑

5. Social bookmark some of the articles you submitted yesterday.

DONE ❑

6. Answer five questions at Yahoo Answers, leaving links in four answers.

DONE ❑

Day 23

1. No new articles to write today! You get a break!

2. Once again, do research to find out how your pages are ranking on Google. Visit Clickbank to see how many click-throughs you have received. Examine the results you are getting. Have you made any sales yet? What do you need to change? What do you need to do more of?

DONE ❏

3. Create three more one-page blogs as we did yesterday with RSS feeds attached.

DONE ❏

4. Rewrite three articles and create posts from them at your WordPress blog. Make sure your keywords are in anchor text and pointing to your article that is ranking the highest.

DONE ❏

5. Ping your WordPress blog URL and RSS feed at Pingomatic.com.

DONE ❏

6. Answer five questions at Yahoo Answers, leaving links in four answers.

DONE ❏

Day 24

1. Write three articles around your keywords and submit to Ezine Articles.

DONE ❑

2. Go to your Squidoo and Hubpages and switch the pictures around.

DONE ❑

3. Social bookmark your new WordPress posts from yesterday.

DONE ❑

4. Social bookmark some of the one-page blogs you created.

DONE ❑

5. Do some forum posting and blog commenting.

DONE ❑

6. Answer five questions at Yahoo Answers, leaving links in four answers.

DONE ❑

Day 25

1. Write three articles around your keywords and submit them to Ezine Articles.

DONE ❏

2. Rewrite three articles and create new post from them at your WordPress blog.

DONE ❏

3. Ping your WordPress URL and RSS feed at Pingomatic.com.

DONE ❏

4. Social bookmark the remaining one-page blogs you created on Day 23.

DONE ❏

5. Do some forum posting and blog commenting.

DONE ❏

6. Answer five questions at Yahoo Answers leaving links in four answers.

❏ DONE

Day 26

1. Write three articles around keywords and submit them to Ezine Articles.

DONE ❏

2. Submit three recently approved articles to the various article directories.

DONE ❏

3. Social bookmark yesterday's posts from your WordPress blog.

DONE ❏

4. Do some forum posting and blog commenting.

DONE ❏

5. Answer five questions at Yahoo Answers, leaving links in four of five answers.

DONE ❏

Day 27

1. Write three articles around keywords and submit them to Ezine Articles.

DONE ❏

2. Go to Squidoo and Hubpages and change the graphics.

DONE ❏

3. Create three more one-page Blogger blogs from articles and add your Ezine Articles author RSS feed, as well as your Hubpage, WordPress.com and Squidoo RSS feeds.

DONE ❏

4. Rewrite three articles and create posts at your WordPress blog.

DONE ❏

5. Ping your WordPress blogs URL and RSS feed at Pingomatic.com.

DONE ❏

6. Answer five questions at Yahoo Answers, leaving links in four answers.

DONE ❏

Day 28

1. Write three articles around keywords and submit them to Ezine Articles.

DONE ❑

2. Social Bookmark yesterday's WordPress blog posts.

DONE ❑

3. Social Bookmark the one-page Blogger blogs you made yesterday.

DONE ❑

4. Do some forum posting and blog commenting for back-links.

DONE ❑

5. Answer five questions at Yahoo Answers, leaving links in four answers.

DONE ❑

Day 29

1. Write three articles around keywords and submit them to Ezine Articles.

DONE ❏

2. Take 3 recently approved articles and submit them to the various article directories you signed up for.

DONE ❏

3. Social Bookmark anything you have not social bookmarked yet.

DONE ❏

4. Create more one-page Blogger blogs including your other RSS feeds on each blog.

DONE ❏

5. Answer five questions at Yahoo Answers, leaving links in four answers.

DONE ❏

Remember to always be checking to see how your articles are doing as far as ranking and click-throughs.

This is extremely important. Do not just do all this blindly. Yes, you will get sales, but you must learn to maximize the potential of a page as well as bring those that are not performing as well up to par.

Day 30

1. Write three articles around keywords and submit them to Ezine Articles.

DONE ❏

2. Rewrite three articles and create posts at your WordPress blog.

DONE ❏

3. Ping your WordPress blog URL and RSS feed at Pingomatic.com.

DONE ❏

4. Go to Squidoo and Hubpages and change the graphics.

DONE ❏

5. Ping your Squidoo and Hubpage at Pingomatic.com.

DONE ❏

6. Answer five questions at Yahoo Answers leaving links in four answers.

DONE ❏

YOU'VE DONE IT!!!

Take a deep breath and congratulate yourself!

Now, pick another niche and repeat the process again.

However, you are not done with this niche just yet. While you may not have to keep up the schedule above, depending on where you are ranking for your keywords, you now have a lot of content in a lot of different places.

The beauty of this process is that you can repeat it over and over and over again. You're probably saying to yourself, how the hell am I going to have the time to do all of that with more than one niche? Remember, outsourcing is affordable and, if you want to be serious about making money online, it is necessary.

PART THREE: Becoming An Even Better Article Marketer (And Make More Money!)

CHAPTER SIX: Make Your Articles Sell Themselves

Common Article Marketing Mistakes

The major reasons most articles fail to produce results is because they have:

1. A weak subject/title/headline

2. A weak summary/description

3. Mediocre content/body

4. A weak call-to-action, closing, resource box

You'll notice that the mistakes listed above are very similar to the mistakes most people make when creating ads and sales letters.

Hot Tip: A great sales letter is very much like an article, and a great article is very much like a sales letter.

Let me rephrase the second part of that sentence. A great article should *not* be "salesy." However, it should have the same important components as a good sales letter.

The subject/headline, description, body, and closer should all be relevant and targeted to the reader. Also, it should inform, educate, even entertain the reader - and then tell him/her what to do, clearly.

Here's the biggest mistake most people make with article marketing:

They let the term "article marketing" limit their imagination, i.e. they only submit "articles" to article directories. Instead, think of it as "content marketing."

Content Marketing

What's the difference between article marketing and content marketing?

Article marketing is just *one part* of content marketing. Content marketing is about recycling and re-using your content in as many different ways as possible. Each new way can bring in more traffic, subscribers, and sales for you, without your having to write a single extra word.

You can take the same articles/content, add your keywords and submit them to the major search engines. If you do it right, this creates more free traffic.

First, let's get the correct 'article marketing' steps down. And, then we'll move on to the other powerful and creative ways of using your content to create lots of free, quality traffic.

Okay…so, how do we avoid the major article marketing mistakes listed earlier, in order to create articles that produce the best possible results for us?

Here are some useful tips to follow:

Title/Headline

If you have studied copywriting at all, think of the tips you've read or heard about creating powerful headlines. Many of the same principles apply here. Your title should:

- Relay a strong benefit to the reader (preferably a specific one.)

- Include 'hot button' words, trance words, or keywords. The reader should immediately recognize what the article is about, and whether or not it relates to him. (These are also the keywords/key phrases that your targeted buyers would be searching online for.)

- Phrase your title in the form of a question, just as many powerful headlines are. Example: "Would you like to improve..." or "Do you make these xyz mistakes...", etc.

Hot Tip: Your headline should appeal to both humans *and* search engines. Here's an easy way to do that:

Place your strong keywords at the beginning (for search engines) then follow with a strong/specific benefit (for humans).

Example: **Fly Fishing - Do You Make These 3 Common Fly Fishing Mistakes?**

Don't be subtle! Get the reader's attention by spicing your headline up a bit. (If you can make it controversial, shocking or outrageous, go for it.)

Remember, your goal is to get their attention, just as you would when creating a powerful ad.

Summary/Description

The summary or description is a short blurb you submit to the article directories. It's like a soft ad for your article. If your summary is interesting and compelling enough, the reader will want to read more.

If your article gets picked up by search engines, your summary/description is what they will display below your headline. Again, this is what will further entice your reader to click on your link, to read the rest of your article.

You want to use powerful keywords in your summary as well, and you also want to offer a powerful benefit.

And, just like with the headline, you can phrase your summary in the form of a question. Then follow up with a promise to answer that question inside the article.

Example: *Would you like to improve your fly fishing results dramatically? In this article, you will learn 3 quick and easy ways to do just that.*

Notice how the first sentence asks a relevant question, and the second one promises to answer it inside.

Body

Just as you would do when creating an effective sales letter, you want to make good use of white space in your article. Keeping the sentences and paragraphs short, with white spaces in between makes the article easy to read. (Your paragraphs should not exceed four to five sentences.)

You can also do this by breaking the content up with the use of bullets, numbers, indents, quotes, etc.

Whenever possible, start your first sentence with your keyword phrase, or at least use the keyword phrase somewhere within the first sentence.

The average length of your entire article should be at least 250 words, and up to 500 words maximum. (Of course, also be mindful of the rules / format requirements of the site to which you are submitting your article and adjust accordingly.)

Give them real value in your article, but always leave them wanting more.

When it comes to layout, your call to action should not be separate from your article. Instead, the article should lead them smoothly into the call to action.

So, rather than ending your article like you normally would, and then placing a resource box or signature file at the end of the article, you should end your article with something like this:

To get 10 more powerful tips on fly fishing, get my free special report from here: 10 Easy Ways To Improve Your Fly Fishing Experience.

(The underlined text would be your link, which contains your keywords as your anchor text.)

You can then include a short blurb about yourself and your main site, after the call to action.

The common mistake most people make is to start talking about themselves, their experience, and their site before the call to action. This interrupts the flow and gets in the way of your reader going to your site.

By using the tip given above, you keep the flow going, and lead readers straight to your site, instead of ending the article, and hoping that they will read your resource box.

Remember, people don't care about who you are or what your resume looks like. Not at this point anyway. Right now, they only care about what they are getting out of the deal. Period.

So, give them what they want. Get them to your site right away and convince them to buy the product you are promoting (or whatever your call to action may be.)

Of course, to make this work, your call to action has to be something they just cannot pass up. As mentioned earlier on, a weak call to action will produce poor (or no) results.

So, make it enticing, make it seductive. Give them great

value in exchange for taking the time to click on your link. <u>Warning:</u> Do NOT promote within the body of the article. That's where you should provide solid content. The call to action is the place to hit them with a powerful offer.

Any Ol' Article Will *Not* Do

Certain types of articles tend to draw more clicks, readers and exposure than others. So it only makes sense to learn about these *proven* formulas and formats for creating articles, and then focus only on those. (Time is our most precious commodity, yes?)

Here then, are the best article formats to use, for maximum results:

- A How-to article: "How to Do XYZ"... "How to Be XYZ"... "How to Have XYZ" etc.

- A steps-focused article: "5 Steps to XYZ ... " (This one is similar to the 'How-to' article.)

- A tips-focused article: "5 Tips for ... " (improving your golf swing, curing athlete's foot, etc.)

- A list-focused article: "Top 5 List of XYZ ... " (places, services, mistakes, snappy comebacks, etc.)

- A review: Here you would basically write a review for a product, service, etc. (Great to use with / promote affiliate programs.)

- A "top mistakes" article: "5 Common XYZ Mistakes

..." ("And How to Avoid Them" etc.)

You can also spice things up by using some of these types:

- 5 Warning Signs...

- 10 Rules of...

- 7 Deadly XYZ Mistakes...

- 5 Questions You Must Ask (Your XYZ... Before You XYZ... etc.)

Yes, you can submit the same article to multiple sites. Always submit articles to article directories first and then add the articles to blogs and other sites. The best authority sites' version will get ranked highest in the search engines anyway.

You will be amazed at the traffic you will start to generate and how very quickly it will happen.

And remember, every article that you submit will continue to work for you indefinitely! It will continue to bring you more and more traffic over time.

Okay, now that we've covered article marketing, it's time to go back and look at the big picture.

Focus on *Content* Marketing

As touched on earlier, don't make the biggest mistake that most marketers make. Don't just use your work as articles that you submit to article directories. You can recycle that same content in many unique and creative ways to turn every single article into an even bigger profit generator.

You can turn your articles into press releases, guest blog posts and special reports (that can go viral). You break up the content (into lessons) and place into an autoresponder series. (More about autoresponders in the next section of this book.)

You can take five to 10 articles for any given niche/subject, turn them into Web articles, do some basic keyword tweaks, and create a hub/content/authority site. Once you start getting free, targeted traffic from search engines, you can even sell these sites for several times what it cost you to create them.

You can sell the content to other article marketers who are looking for articles. You can sell the special reports, audios and videos created from these articles as well.

(While you may not want to sell the content that you're using yourself, know it is a money-making option you have. If you do go this route, let your customers know that you are already using the content "as is" yourself.)

PART FOUR: The Money Is In the List

CHAPTER SEVEN: Your Most Powerful Money-Making Tool: How to Build a Mailing List

Throughout this book you have been instructed to follow a method of article marketing that was meant to help you ease into your new business venture as quickly as possible and as uncomplicated as possible.

Now that you've put in the hours to learn the basics, write your own articles and create a content funnel, it's time learn a few other techniques that will take your article marketing to the next level.

The Value Is In the List

Earlier in the book, you were given the instruction to take the affiliate link you acquired from Clickbank (when you chose the product you wanted promote), buy a domain name, and forward your domain name to your affiliate link. Using this method would bring anyone who clicked on your link directly to the product page.

While this method is simple, there is another method which will take a bit more time to set up, but in the end, will be much more profitable for you.

All successful Internet marketers have achieved their greatest success by establishing a relationship with the people they connect with through their articles. When you direct an article reader to a product page, while you might get a sale, you are not establishing a relationship with them. In fact, you are actually helping the product creator to establish a relationship while you, on the other hand, continue to find new potential customers.

The benefit of having a relationship with your article readers is that you will have the opportunity to build trust with them. The more trust you have built, the more likely they will buy from you, not once, but multiple times.

So, how do you establish a relationship with those who have read one of your articles? You invite them to sign up for your mailing list.

Once someone has signed up for your mailing list, they have given you permission to contact them with more information. They are telling you they are interested in what you have to offer. Now, you have the chance to speak to them directly and send them good, quality content they will appreciate.

The benefits of having people sign up for your mailing list are numerous. Most importantly, having a mailing list will save you a great deal of time. Rather than spending hours continuing to build your content funnel to get one-off sales, you can send out a well-written e-mail to people who are eager, and expecting, to hear from you. Depending on how many people are on your list, one email can generate many sales.

When you are using an affiliate link to generate sales, you are promoting one product. But, as you have probably noticed during your visits to Clickbank, there are several products being sold within the niche you chose. Having a mailing list will enable you to promote not only one product, but various products within this niche. Often times, when people are looking for a solution to a problem, they want to check out various sources of information. With your mailing list, you have the opportunity to educate them on what products are out there and encourage them to check out the ones you feel good about promoting.

Once you build your mailing list, things can get very exciting. Not only does it give you direct access to hungry buyers, but you can also contact product creators directly to partner with them to promote their products. This means more income opportunities for you. In fact, there may come a day when you decide to create your own product. Once you do, you can announce it to your mailing list directly and bypass spending hours upon hours promoting it via article marketing.

I'm not suggesting having a mailing list will take away the need to build your content funnel. It will be one arm of your online marketing business—albeit a very powerful one.

Setting Up Your Mailing List

Your mailing list is going to be one of the most valuable assets belonging to your online business. Because of this, you have to entrust a reputable company that specializes in mailing list services.

Over the years, I have used Aweber.com with great success. While there are other companies out there, Aweber has been around the longest. They also have many tools to help you create an email that will, not only get to the receiver (without being flagged as spam), but also opened by the receiver. They also have extensive tracking stats so you can see how many people opened the e-mail and how many clicked on the link inside.

There is a monthly fee (between $20 and $30). Within this book, I have attempted to give you free options to help you get your article marketing started without the worry of money. However, along with investing in a few domain names, I highly recommend investing in a monthly mailing list service. If used properly and intelligently, the mailing list will pay for itself tenfold.

No matter what service you use, each site will have tutorials showing you how to set up your mailing list. Once you have done so, you will need the HTML code for what is known as the "opt-in form." This is the box you have no doubt seen on Web sites in which you type in your name and your email address and click on a button that might say "Join" or "Submit."

You can customize the opt-in box to collect whatever information you desire. Most Web visitors are used to the simple name/email address format.

Once you have the HTML code for your mailing list, what do you do with it? You put it on something called a "landing page."

Creating a Landing Page

Previously, when you researched already high-ranking articles doing well in your niche, you clicked on links found in each article's resource box. You probably remember noting how each article marketer approached things differently. Some of them had a link pointing to a product, while others had a link pointing to a landing page.

It would be worth your time to go back and look over the landing pages these marketers created to get ideas for yours.

While there are some marketers who have their landing page on sites like Blogger, it is wiser to host it on your own site. Again, you will need a domain name and a Web host for this. The good news is a landing page will be a basic Web design that does not take a lot of time to create or set up.

Your landing page is like a pre-sales page to the product. It needs to contain an attention-grabbing headline, copy that speaks to the visitor and some bullet points which give the visitor an idea of the benefits they will receive from the product.

Once you have given product details, instead of including a link to the product itself, you will place your opt-in box.

Above your opt-in box, tell the visitor you would like to send them free information that pertains to the problem they are having. As an example, if your niche is "leash training your dog" and the product you are promoting is an ebook teaching how to leash train in 10 easy steps, to entice your reader to sign up for your mailing list, offer them three free tips on leash training.

A mistake marketers often make is to tell people to sign up for their mailing list without giving them an incentive to do so. Years ago, when people were just getting to know the Web, getting emails was an exciting thing. People would sign up for many mailing lists. These days, people are leery of their email being passed along to spammers. Also, the novelty of receiving emails has dissolved. These days, people want a good reason to give their email address to a total stranger. You have to respect that and give them something valuable (in the form of quality, useful content) in exchange for their trust.

Again, the landing page need only contain a headline, information about the product to pique the curiosity of the visitor, your opt-in box and your offer of free goodies in exchange for their email address.

Having a landing page changes the dynamic of your content funnel. Up until this point, all of your articles, blog posts, forum comments, etc. were all used to bring the reader to the article you wanted to rank high on Google. If you have a well-crafted landing page, this now becomes the page you will send all your traffic to and the page you want to rank high. Rather than including your affiliate link, the link to your landing page will be the one you include in your article resource box and the link you include whenever you post an article anywhere.

Once the visitor is signed up to your mailing list, then you send along your affiliate link in an attempt to make a sale.

Talking to Your List

Even before you have subscribers signing up for your mailing list, you need to set up what is known as an "autoresponder." This is a series of emails that is sent out immediately after someone signs up.

Assuming you choose one of the better mailing list service providers, you will have the ability to upload an email and set it for a specific time it is sent out. Again, using the leash training tips as an example, your autoresponder series would look something like this:

- A welcome e-mail would be sent out right after the visitor has subscribed.

- A second email would be sent right after containing Tip #1.

- The next day, an email containing Tip #2 would be sent.

- On the third day, Tip #3 would be sent out along with information about the product you are promoting along with your affiliate link.

After this series of emails, it is up to you how often you stay in touch with your mailing list. You may want to schedule an exclusive article to be sent to your mailing list every Friday. Or, you may want to create an email newsletter containing information about your niche (product reviews, news, how-to articles) which is sent out once a month. It is your choice.

The two biggest mistakes marketers make are to either only send out emails when they have something to promote or they do not stay in touch with your list on a regular basis. Do not make these mistakes. Build a relationship with your subscribers by contacting them in a reasonable fashion and always leaving them feel that you care about their problem and their interest in your niche.

Using Your Mailing List to Get Ideas

Finally, utilize your mailing list to learn about your subscribers and what they want. Ask them to send you feedback on your articles and to let you know what their biggest concerns are when it comes to the problem that lead them to find you in the first place. Feedback and take the form of reply e-mails or having them fill out a survey. (SurveyMonkey.com lets you create free surveys.)

Your subscribers can give you ideas for new articles or even future products you could create and sell to them. They can give you feedback on the quality of any of your marketing ideas and the changes you need to make.

As previously mentioned, having a mailing list of people you can be in direct contact with is the most powerful tool you can have.

While this is a general overview of setting up a mailing list, the hope is that it has inspired you to think beyond article marketing and see you have so much more to offer.

CONCLUSION

The person that's making 10, 100, or even a 1000 times more money than you right now gets only 24 hours each day just as you do and not a second more.

The only reason they are able to make more money is because they are using the best strategies that allow them to leverage their resources.

Do you want to know what the difference between you and a top guru marketer is?

It's *time*. That's the only difference. The guru marketers just got an earlier start than you.

How can you get the kind of results they are getting? By starting with one article. Just like the gurus did.

These are just regular people who took action. They started with one article, one submission, and they kept going. They learned the strategies, and they worked to create a "system" that is now working for them – and will continue to work for many, many years. Maybe even for the rest of their lives.

But, it all started with one single article, one single subscriber, one single sale and eventually turned into automatic, unstoppable profits.

So, please put the work in right now. Several months from now, you can look back on this moment as being the day that you changed your financial future dramatically – for

the better.
I wish you great success!

Mike Stapleton

For more information about article marketing and to learn
the most up to date article marketing techniques, visit my
Web site: **mikesmoneymethod.com**

LaVergne, TN USA
13 October 2010
200676LV00002B/84/P